FINGER TWISTER TRICKS

Classic, Cr...

978-1-913174-06-4

Copyright Bell & Mackenzie Publishing Limited 2019

This book contains adapted text and images from the book
String Figures And How To Make Them by Caroline Furness
Jayne first published in 1906

INFORMATION ?

Are you ready to impress with some amazing, crazy, string art?

Creating cool shapes from string is great fun and once you've mastered the moves you'll be the envy of all your friends. You might be new to string art but it's actually been around for a long time. Your mum and dad will recognise it, your grandparents and probably even their parents too! The tricks in this book are over 100 years old and kids the world over have been making them and perfecting their skills for generations.

As with any skill though, it takes time and LOTS of practice to perfect your art. At first glance the tricks won't look as easy as you might like, but don't be put off. Read each step of the instructions over and over, one sentence at a time until you understand the step. You'll make mistakes, lots of them and literally get tied in knots sometimes but you WILL get it if you keep trying. The reward will be looks of amazement from friends and family as you show them your cool creations.

To help you really learn the tricks, all the hand diagrams include very detailed instructions. Sometimes it will be enough to just look at the pictures and follow them.... but in case you get stuck, ask an adult to read out the instructions to you carefully to help you work it out. It takes time, patience and a little bit of skill, but if you stick with it you'll be an expert in no time.

Some of the tricks in this book can be easier to master, like: **Circle, Witches Broom**, **Cooking Pot** & **Waterfall** - so if you're new to string art, start with these. Also included are some really tricky ones like **Wigwam** and the original version of **Jacobs Ladder**, which used to be called 'Osage Diamonds' and comes from the Native American culture. Plus there are also some tricks like **Pretty Diamonds** where you'll need the help of a friend as an extra pair of hands.

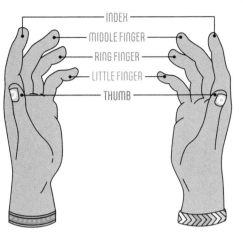

It can be tricky to explain each step and the language used will at first feel unfamiliar so, to help you work it out, all the fingers on your hands have been named so you know which finger (digit) to use. You'll also notice that some of the patterns have the words '**palmar**' string and '**dorsal**' string.

A string lying across the palm of the hand is a **palmar** string
A string lying across the back of the hand is a **dorsal** string. Simple!

Lets get started.....

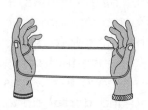

FIGURE A

FIGURE B

FIGURE C

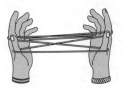

FIGURE D

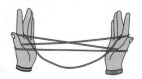

FIGURE E

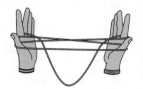

FIGURE F

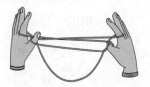

FIGURE G

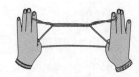

FIGURE H

STEP ONE

Put the little fingers into the loop of string, and separate the hands. You now have a single loop on each little finger passing directly to the opposite little finger.

Turning the hands with the palms away from you, put each thumb into the little finger loop from below, and pick up on the back of the thumb the near little finger string; then, allowing the far little finger string to remain on the little finger, turn the hands with the palms facing each other, return the thumbs to their extended position, and draw the strings tight **(Fig. A)**.

STEP TWO

Bring the hands together, and put the right index up under the string which crosses the left palm **(Fig. B)**, and draw the loop out on the back of the finger by separating the hands.

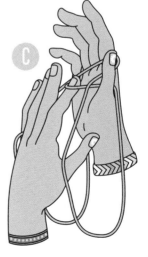

STEP THREE

Bring the hands together again, and put the left index up under that part of the string crossing the palm of the right hand which is between the strings on the right index **(Fig. C)**, and draw the loop out on the back of the left index by separating the hands.

STEP FOUR

You now have a loop on each thumb, index, and little finger **(Fig. D)**. There is a near thumb string and a far little finger string passing directly from one hand to the other, and two crosses formed between them by the near little finger string of one hand becoming the far index string of the other hand, and the far thumb string of one hand becoming the near index string of the other hand.

STEP FIVE

Release the loops from the little fingers, but do not separate the hands; let the long loop hang down **(Fig. E)**.

STEP SIX

Toss this long loop toward you over all the other strings and let it hang down on the near side **(Fig. F)**.

6

STEP SEVEN

Bend each thumb down into its own loop, over that part of the string of
the hanging loop which crosses over the thumb loop **(Fig. G, left hand)**,
and let the original thumb loop slip over the knuckle and off the thumb
(Fig. G, right hand). Then turn the hands with the palms away from you
and, drawing the strings tight, extend the figure between the thumbs
and index fingers **(Fig. H)**.

WITCHES BROOM

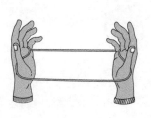

FIGURE **A**

FIGURE **B**

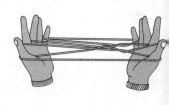

FIGURE **C**

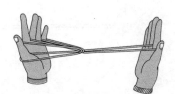

FIGURE **D**

STEP ONE

Put the little fingers into the loop of string, and separate the hands. You now have a single loop on each little finger passing directly to the opposite little finger.

Turning the hands with the palms away from you, put each thumb into the little finger loop from below, and pick up on the back of the thumb the near little finger string; then, allowing the far little finger string to remain on the little finger, turn the hands with the palms facing each other, return the thumbs to their extended position, and draw the strings tight **(Fig. A)**.

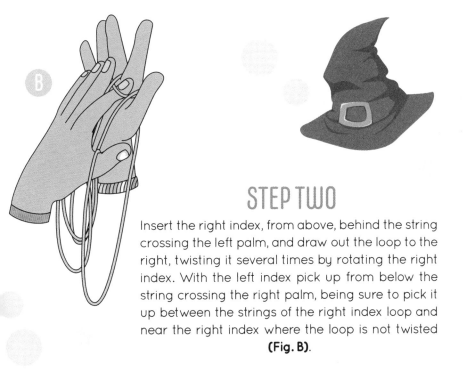

STEP TWO

Insert the right index, from above, behind the string crossing the left palm, and draw out the loop to the right, twisting it several times by rotating the right index. With the left index pick up from below the string crossing the right palm, being sure to pick it up between the strings of the right index loop and near the right index where the loop is not twisted **(Fig. B)**.

WITCHES BROOM

STEP THREE

Separate the hands and draw the strings tight **(Fig. C)**.

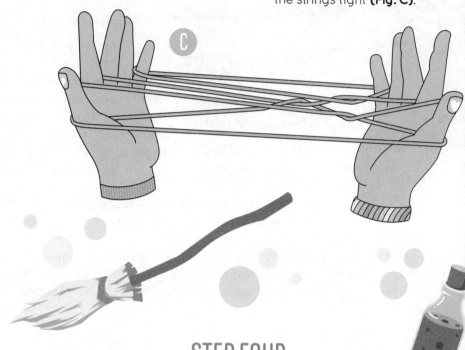

STEP FOUR

Release the loops from the right thumb and little finger, and separate the hands. The brush of the broom will be on the thumb, index, and little finger of the left hand. and the handle will be held by the index of the right hand **(Fig. D)**.

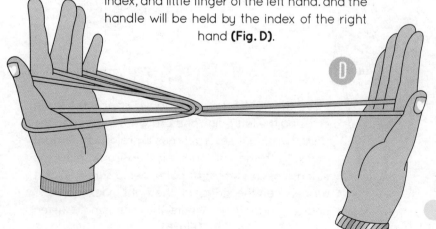

CIRCLE

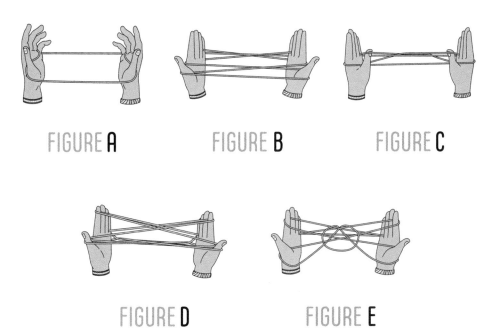

FIGURE **A**

FIGURE **B**

FIGURE **C**

FIGURE **D**

FIGURE **E**

STEP ONE

Put the little fingers into the loop of string, and separate the hands. You now have a single loop on each little finger passing directly and uncrossed to the opposite little finger.

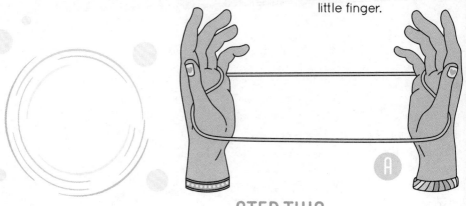

STEP TWO

Turning the hands with the palms away from you, put each thumb into the little finger loop from below, and pick up on the back of the thumb the near little finger string; then, allowing the far little finger string to remain on the little finger, turn the hands with the palms facing each other, return the thumbs to their extended position, and draw the strings tight **(Fig. A)**.

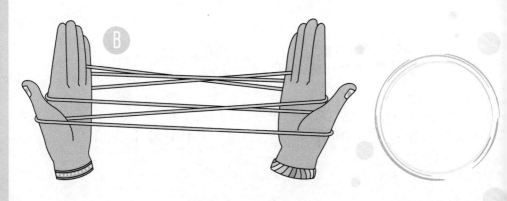

STEP THREE

Pass the right index, middle, ring and little fingers from below, behind the left palmar string, and draw the loop out. Pass the left index, middle, ring and little fingers, from below, behind the right palmar strings; draw the loop out and separate the hands. **(Fig. B)**.

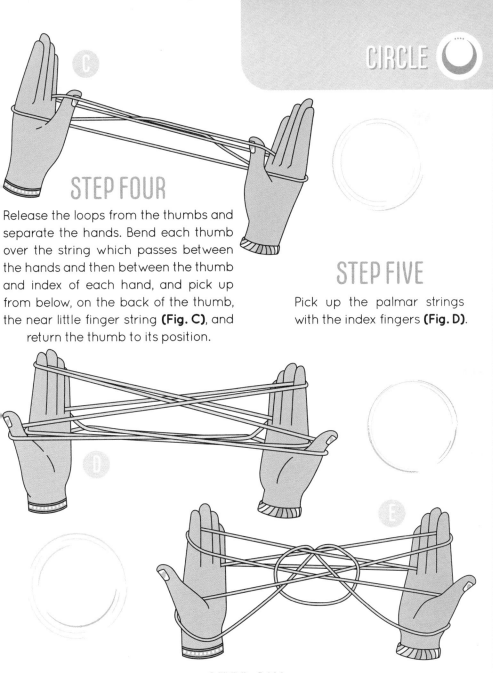

STEP FOUR

Release the loops from the thumbs and separate the hands. Bend each thumb over the string which passes between the hands and then between the thumb and index of each hand, and pick up from below, on the back of the thumb, the near little finger string **(Fig. C)**, and return the thumb to its position.

STEP FIVE

Pick up the palmar strings with the index fingers **(Fig. D)**.

STEP SIX

With the thumb and index of the right hand pick up the string on the back of the left hand, lift it over the tips of the left fingers, and let it drop on the palmar side. With the thumb and index of the left hand pick up the string on the back of the right hand, lift it over the tips of the right fingers, and let it drop on the palmar side. Draw the hands apart and the central circle will appear **(Fig. E)**.

13

FIGURE A

FIGURE B

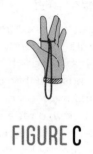

FIGURE C

FIGURE D

FIGURE E

FIGURE F

FIGURE G

FIGURE H

FIGURE I

WATERFALL

STEP ONE

Hold the left hand with the fingers pointing upward and the palm slightly toward you. With the right hand arrange a part of the loop upon the left hand so that it crosses the backs of both index and middle fingers, and passes to the palmar side between the middle and ring finger, and between the index and thumb; let the rest of the loop hang down on the palm **(Fig. A)**.

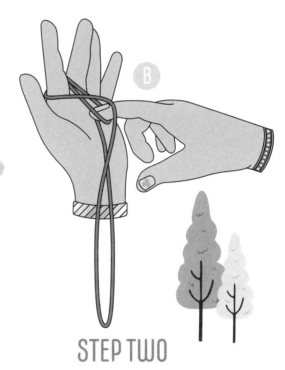

STEP TWO

Put the right index from the near side under the left near index hanging string, and then through between the index and middle finger, and with the ball of the finger pick up the cross string which is on the backs of the left index and middle finger, and pull it through between these fingers **(Fig. B)**, and then out all the way **(Fig. C)**.

15

STEP THREE

Letting the loop hang down on the left palm, put the whole right hand from the near side under the near string and into the hanging loop. Then with the right thumb and index catch, above the string crossing the palmar surfaces of the index and middle finger, the two strings which come from between the left index and middle finger **(Fig. D)**, and draw them out to the right **(Fig. E)** as far as possible. In this movement the loop which hung on the right wrist slips over the right hand and along the two strings just drawn out, until it reaches the palm.

STEP FOUR

You now have on the left hand a loop on the index and a loop on the middle finger, both loops knotted together lower down on the palm **(Fig. F)**. Arrange the four strings which hang down on the palm below the knot so that they lie side by side evenly and uncrossed, with the two which pass up through the knot and between the index and middle finger lying in the middle between the other two. Look carefully and you'll notice that the near string runs up to the knot, passes from the front around a cross string, comes forward, and passes to the far side as a second cross string over all four hanging strings; it then passes from behind around the back cross string, and hangs down in front as the far string of the four.

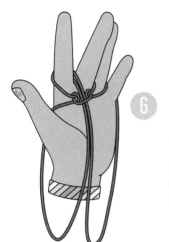

STEP FIVE

With the thumb and index of the right hand pick up, below the knot, the near hanging string, and put it behind the left thumb; then pick up the far hanging string, and put it behind the little finger **(Fig. G)**.

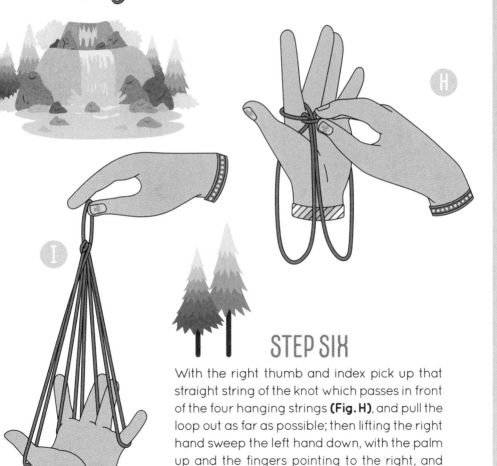

STEP SIX

With the right thumb and index pick up that straight string of the knot which passes in front of the four hanging strings **(Fig. H)**, and pull the loop out as far as possible; then lifting the right hand sweep the left hand down, with the palm up and the fingers pointing to the right, and draw the strings moderately tight, and you will form a waterfall **(Fig. I)**.

FIGURE **A**

FIGURE **B**

FIGURE **C**

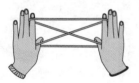

FIGURE **D**

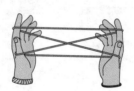

FIGURE **E**

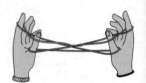

FIGURE **F**

FIGURE **G**

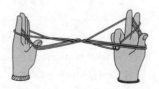

FIGURE **H**

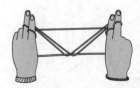

FIGURE **I**

STEP ONE

Hold the string between the tips of the thumb and index of each hand, so that a short piece passes between the hands and a long loop hangs down. Make a small ring, hanging down, in the short string, putting the right hand string away from you over the left hand string **(Fig. A)**.

STEP TWO

Insert the index fingers into the ring downward and toward you **(Fig. B)**, and, putting the thumbs away from you into the long hanging loop **(Fig. C)**,

THE BOW

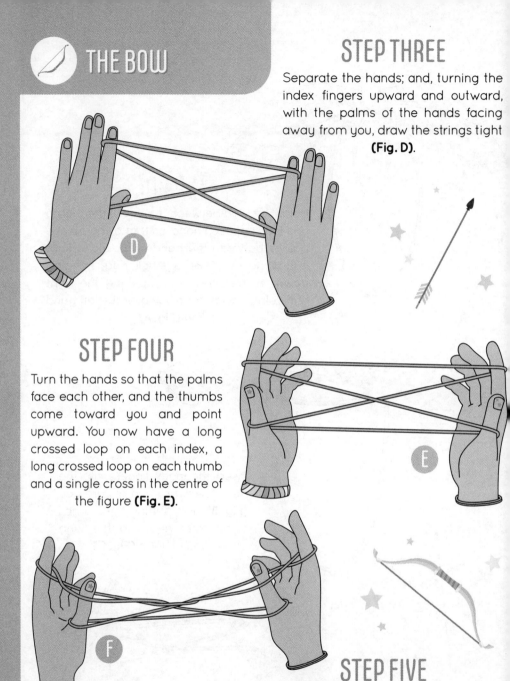

STEP THREE

Separate the hands; and, turning the index fingers upward and outward, with the palms of the hands facing away from you, draw the strings tight **(Fig. D)**.

STEP FOUR

Turn the hands so that the palms face each other, and the thumbs come toward you and point upward. You now have a long crossed loop on each index, a long crossed loop on each thumb and a single cross in the centre of the figure **(Fig. E)**.

STEP FIVE

Pass each thumb away from you over the near index string, and take up from below with the back of the thumb the far index string, and return the thumb to its former position **(Fig. F)**. This movement draws the far index string over the near index string.

STEP SIX

Pass each middle finger toward you over the near index string, and take up from below on the back of the finger the far thumb string **(Fig. G, left hand)**, and return the middle finger to its original position **(Fig. G, right hand)**.

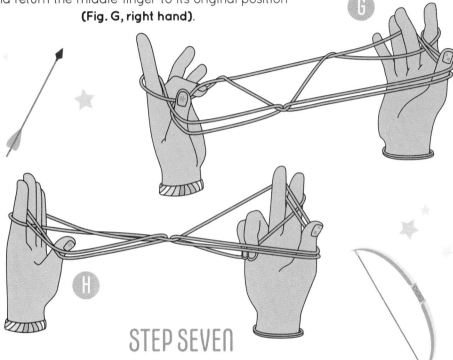

STEP SEVEN

Turn the palms toward you, and put the ring and little fingers of each hand from below between the near index string and the far middle finger string **(Fig. H, left hand)**, and pull down the near index string by closing the ring and little fingers on the palm **(Fig. H, right hand)**.

STEP EIGHT

Keep the index and middle fingers erect; release the loops from the thumbs, and turn the palms away from you, drawing the strings tight **(Fig. I)**.

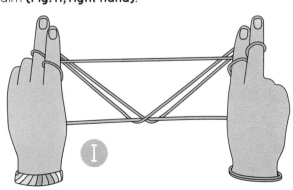

FIGURE A

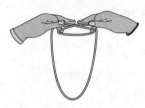

FIGURE B

FIGURE C

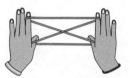

FIGURE D

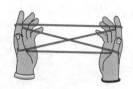

FIGURE E

FIGURE F

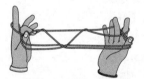

FIGURE G

FIGURE H

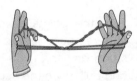

FIGURE I

FIGURE J

FIGURE K

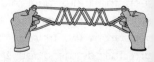

FIGURE L

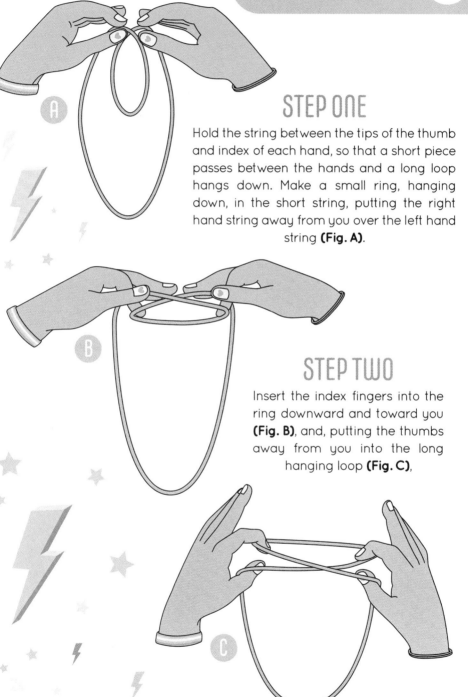

STEP ONE

Hold the string between the tips of the thumb and index of each hand, so that a short piece passes between the hands and a long loop hangs down. Make a small ring, hanging down, in the short string, putting the right hand string away from you over the left hand string **(Fig. A)**.

STEP TWO

Insert the index fingers into the ring downward and toward you **(Fig. B)**, and, putting the thumbs away from you into the long hanging loop **(Fig. C)**,

STEP THREE

Separate the hands; and, turning the index fingers upward and outward, with the palms of the hands facing away from you, draw the strings tight **(Fig. D)**.

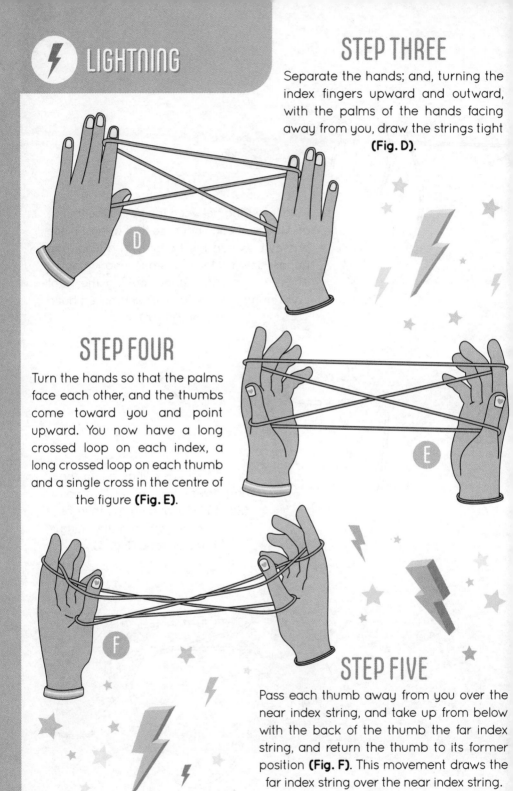

STEP FOUR

Turn the hands so that the palms face each other, and the thumbs come toward you and point upward. You now have a long crossed loop on each index, a long crossed loop on each thumb and a single cross in the centre of the figure **(Fig. E)**.

STEP FIVE

Pass each thumb away from you over the near index string, and take up from below with the back of the thumb the far index string, and return the thumb to its former position **(Fig. F)**. This movement draws the far index string over the near index string.

STEP SIX

Pass each middle finger toward you over the near index string, and take up from below on the back of the finger the far thumb string **(Fig. G, left hand)**, and return the middle finger to its original position **(Fig. G, right hand)**.

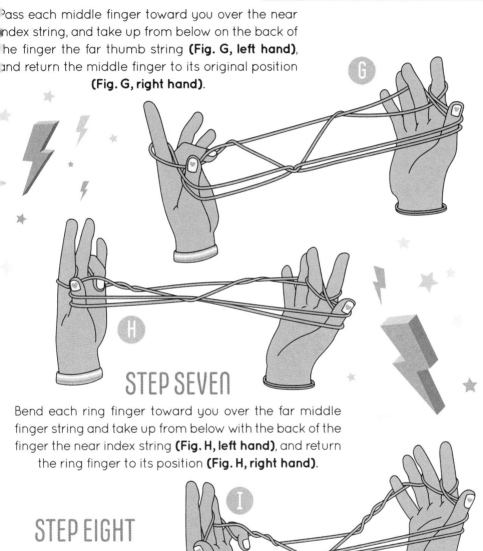

STEP SEVEN

Bend each ring finger toward you over the far middle finger string and take up from below with the back of the finger the near index string **(Fig. H, left hand)**, and return the ring finger to its position **(Fig. H, right hand)**.

STEP EIGHT

Pass each little finger over the far ring finger string, and take up from below on the back of the finger the far middle finger string **(Fig. I, left hand)**, and return the little finger to its position **(Fig. I, right hand)**.

You now have two twisted strings passing between the two little fingers, two loose strings passing over the thumbs and two strings laced around the other fingers.

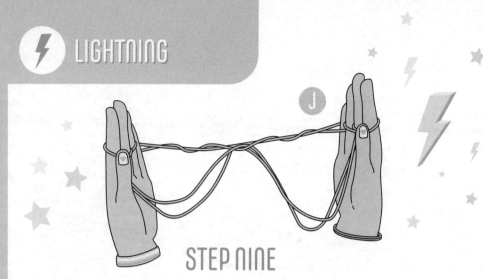

STEP NINE

Turn the hands with the thumbs upward and the palms facing each other. The little finger strings should be tight, but must not be disturbed. Keep all the fingers close together so that the strings cannot slip; the success of the figure depends entirely on this. Take the thumbs out of their loops **(Fig. J)**, and throw these loops away from you over the tightly drawn twisted little finger strings **(Fig. K)**.

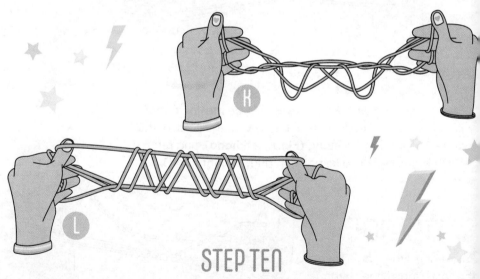

STEP TEN

Insert each thumb into the small space between the twisted little finger strings, close to the little finger, and lift up the upper of the two strings (the far ring finger string). Now, if the lower string is kept tightly drawn and the other fingers kept close together, the loose hanging strings (the original thumb loops) will become wrapped around the twisted little finger strings as these gradually untwist when the upper string is lifted by the thumb. This movement forms the figure, which should be about two inches high **(Fig. L)**.

RABBIT

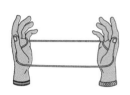

FIGURE **A**

FIGURE **B**

FIGURE **C**

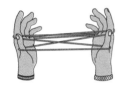

FIGURE **D**

FIGURE **E**

FIGURE **F**

FIGURE **G**

FIGURE **H**

FIGURE **I**

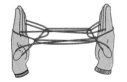

FIGURE **J**

FIGURE **K**

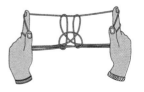

FIGURE **L**

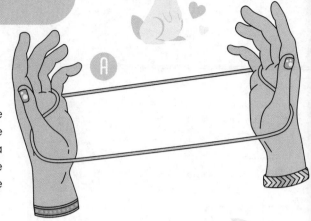

STEP ONE

Put the little fingers into the loop of string, and separate the hands. You now have a single loop on each little finger passing directly to the opposite little finger.

Turning the hands with the palms away from you, put each thumb into the little finger loop from below, and pick up on the back of the thumb the near little finger string; then, allowing the far little finger string to remain on the little finger, turn the hands with the palms facing each other, return the thumbs to their extended position, and draw the strings tight **(Fig. A)**.

STEP TWO

Bring the hands together, and put the right index up under the string which crosses the left palm **(Fig. B)**, and draw the loop out on the back of the finger by separating the hands.

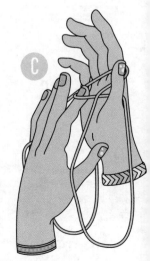

STEP THREE

Bring the hands together again, and put the left index up under that part of the string crossing the palm of the right hand which is between the strings on the right index **(Fig. C)**, and draw the loop out on the back of the left index by separating the hands.

STEP FOUR

You now have a loop on each thumb, index, and little finger **(Fig. D)**. There is a near thumb string and a far little finger string passing directly from one hand to the other, and two crosses formed between them by the near little finger string of one hand becoming the far index string of the other hand, and the far thumb string of one hand becoming the near index string of the other hand.

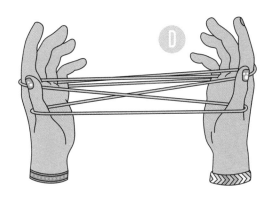

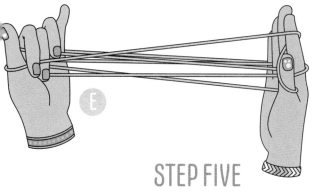

STEP FIVE

Bend each middle finger down toward you into the thumb loop, and bend each index down toward you on the near side of the near thumb string **(Fig. E, left hand)**, then, holding this string tightly between these two fingers, straighten the fingers and turn the palms away from you to put the string around the tip of the index **(Fig. E, right hand)**. Release the loops from the thumbs.

STEP SIX

Pass each thumb from below into the little finger loop and draw toward you, on the back of the thumb, the near little finger, the upper far index string and both strings of the lower index loop **(Fig. F)**.

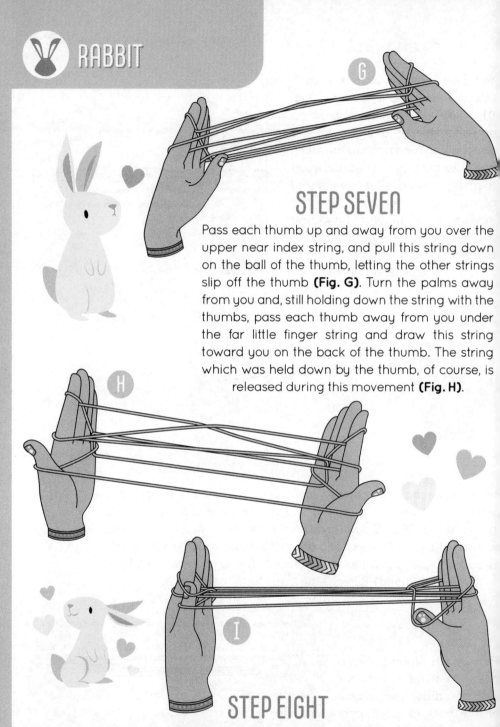

STEP SEVEN

Pass each thumb up and away from you over the upper near index string, and pull this string down on the ball of the thumb, letting the other strings slip off the thumb **(Fig. G)**. Turn the palms away from you and, still holding down the string with the thumbs, pass each thumb away from you under the far little finger string and draw this string toward you on the back of the thumb. The string which was held down by the thumb, of course, is released during this movement **(Fig. H)**.

STEP EIGHT

Insert each thumb from below (close to the index) into the small ring-like upper index loop **(Fig. I, left hand)** and draw the upper near index string, on the back of the thumb, down through the thumb loop, this latter loop slipping off the thumb during the movement **(Fig. I, right hand)**.

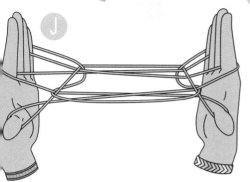

STEP NINE

Release the upper loop from each index **(Fig. J)**.

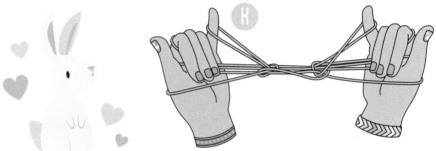

STEP TEN

Pass the index, middle and ring fingers of each hand toward you and down into the thumb loop **(Fig. K)**; then gently release the loops from the little fingers, and put each little finger toward you in the loop with the ring, middle and index fingers. Hold all four fingers of each hand down on the palm; turn the hands with the palms facing each other. Lift up the near thumb string on the tip of each index, and withdraw the thumb. Some working of the strings is usually required to make the "Rabbit" appear **(Fig. L)**.

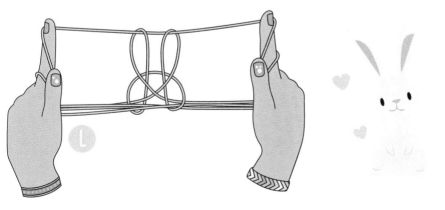

FIGURE **A**

FIGURE **B**

FIGURE **C**

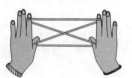

FIGURE **D**

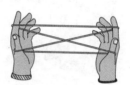

FIGURE **E**

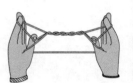

FIGURE **F**

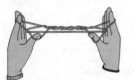

FIGURE **G**

FIGURE **H**

FIGURE **I**

FIGURE **J**

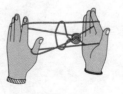

FIGURE **K**

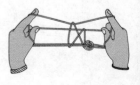

FIGURE **L**

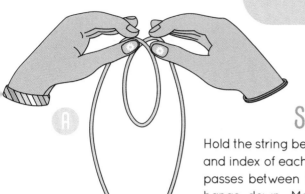

STEP ONE

Hold the string between the tips of the thumb and index of each hand, so that a short piece passes between the hands and a long loop hangs down. Make a small ring, hanging down, in the short string, putting the right hand string away from you over the left hand string **(Fig. A)**.

STEP TWO

Insert the index fingers into the ring downward and toward you **(Fig. B)**, and, putting the thumbs away from you into the long hanging loop **(Fig. C)**,

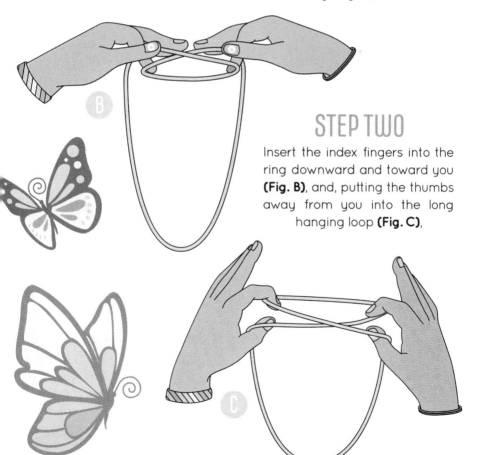

 **BUTTERFLY**

STEP THREE

Separate the hands; and, turning the index fingers upward and outward, with the palms of the hands facing away from you, draw the strings tight **(Fig. D)**.

STEP FOUR

Turn the hands so that the palms face each other, and the thumbs come toward you and point upward. You now have a long crossed loop on each index, a long crossed loop on each thumb and a single cross in the centre of the figure **(Fig. E)**.

STEP FIVE

Twist each index loop five times by rotating each index down toward you, and up again five times. Put each thumb from below into the index loop and, without removing the index, separate the thumb from the index **(Fig. F)**.

34

STEP SIX

On each hand in turn, using your teeth slip the lower (the original) thumb loop over the loop passing around both thumb and index, then entirely off the thumb, and let it drop to the palmar side. Separate the hands **(Fig. G)**.

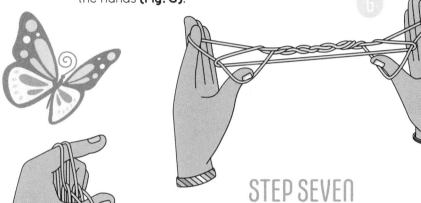

STEP SEVEN

Bring the hands close together, with the index finger and thumb of the one hand pointing toward the index finger and thumb of the other hand; then hang the right index loop on the left index, and the right thumb loop on the left thumb **(Fig. H)**.

STEP EIGHT

Take up with the right index, from the left side, the loop you have just put on the left thumb, and take up with the right thumb, from the right side, the loop which was originally on the left thumb **(Fig. I)**.

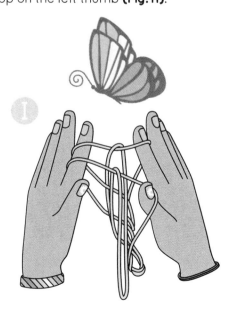

35

BUTTERFLY

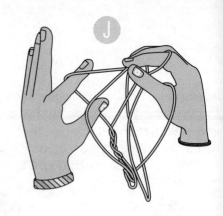

STEP NINE

With the right thumb and index lift both loops from the left index, and put the left index away from you into the loop just hung on the left index, and put the left thumb toward you into the loop originally on the left thumb **(Fig. J)**.

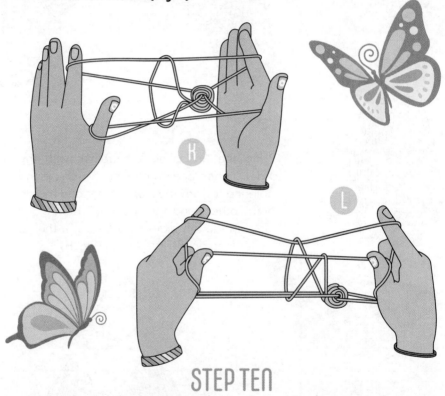

STEP TEN

Now, placing the hands with the thumbs up and the fingers pointing away from you, draw them slowly apart, and when the strings have partially rolled up in the middle of the figure **(Fig. K)**, pull down with the middle, ring and little fingers of each hand the far index string and the near thumb string **(Fig. L)**, and the wings of the butterfly will be held up by the strings extended between the widely separated thumbs and index fingers, and the butterfly's curled tongue will appear rolled up on the strings held down by the other fingers.

TWO STARS

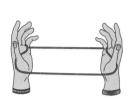

FIGURE **A**

FIGURE **B**

FIGURE **C**

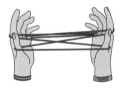

FIGURE **D**

FIGURE **E**

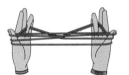

FIGURE **F**

FIGURE **G**

FIGURE **H**

FIGURE **I**

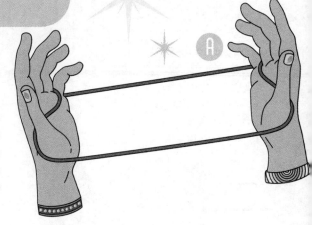

STEP ONE

Put the little fingers into the loop of string, and separate the hands. You now have a single loop on each little finger passing directly to the opposite little finger.

Turning the hands with the palms away from you, put each thumb into the little finger loop from below, and pick up on the back of the thumb the near little finger string; then, allowing the far little finger string to remain on the little finger, turn the hands with the palms facing each other, return the thumbs to their extended position, and draw the strings tight **(Fig. A)**.

STEP TWO

Bring the hands together, and put the right index up under the string which crosses the left palm **(Fig. B)**, and draw the loop out on the back of the finger by separating the hands.

STEP THREE

Bring the hands together again, and put the left index up under that part of the string crossing the palm of the right hand which is between the strings on the right index **(Fig. C)**, and draw the loop out on the back of the left index by separating the hands.

STEP FOUR

You now have a loop on each thumb, index, and little finger **(Fig. D)**. There is a near thumb string and a far little finger string passing directly from one hand to the other, and two crosses formed between them by the near little finger string of one hand becoming the far index string of the other hand, and the far thumb string of one hand becoming the near index string of the other hand.

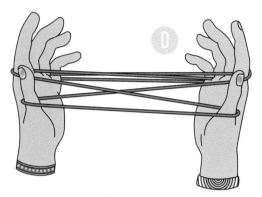

STEP FIVE

Transfer the index loops to the thumbs, by putting each thumb from below into the index loop, withdrawing the index, and returning the thumb to its position.

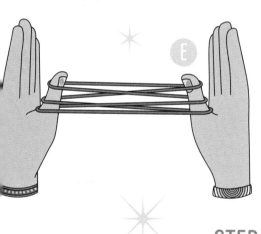

STEP SIX

Transfer the little finger loops to the thumbs, by bending each thumb away from you over the far thumb strings, and taking up from below on the back of the thumb the near little finger string; and then withdrawing the little finger, return the thumb to its position.

You now have three loops on each thumb **(Fig. E)**. Keep them well separated on the thumb: the original loop down at the base, the loop taken from the index halfway up, and the loop taken from the little finger near the tip.

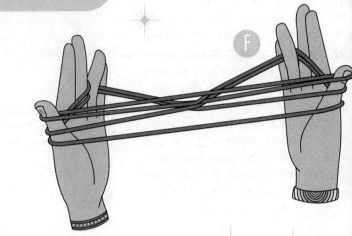

STEP SEVEN

Put each ring finger from below through the two lower thumb loops, and, pushing the two lower far strings away from you with the back of this finger **(Fig. F)**.

STEP EIGHT

Bend the ring finger toward you over the upper far thumb string (the far string which passes directly from thumb to thumb), draw it down, and hold it by closing the ring and little fingers over it on the palm **(Fig. G)**.

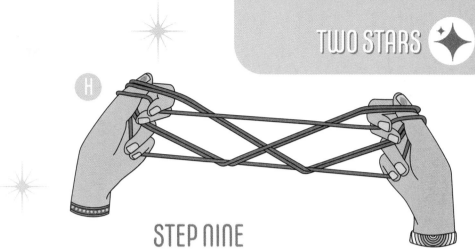

STEP NINE

Turn the hands so that the thumbs, index fingers and middle fingers point away from you; then bending the index and middle finger pass the middle finger toward you through the thumb loops, and pass the index toward you into the two upper thumb loops and then between the two upper near thumb strings and the lower near thumb string (the near string which passes directly from thumb to thumb) **(Fig. H)**. Now, holding this lower near thumb string between the index and middle finger, draw these fingers away from you, and, by turning the index down and then away from you, take the string up on the tip of the finger.

STEP TEN

Release the loops from the thumbs, and, turning the palms away from you, extend the figure between the index fingers and the ring and little fingers closed on the palm **(Fig. I)**.

PRETTY DIAMONDS

You'll need a friend for this trick!

FIGURE **A**

FIGURE **B**

FIGURE **C**

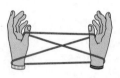

FIGURE **D**

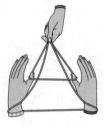

FIGURE **E**

FIGURE **F**

FIGURE **G**

FIGURE **H**

FIGURE **I**

FIGURE **J**

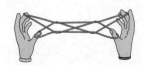

FIGURE **K**

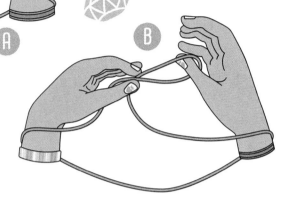

STEP ONE

Put both hands through the loop of string, up to the wrists, and take up between the thumb and index of each hand a short piece of the upper wrist string. Then make a small hanging ring in this string, by passing the string held by the right hand toward you over the left hand string **(Fig. A)**.

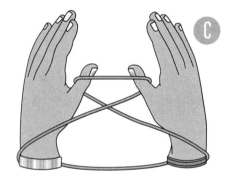

STEP TWO

Turn this ring up, and put first the right thumb **(Fig. B)** and then the left thumb **(Fig. C)** away from you into the ring, and separate the hands **(Fig. D)**.

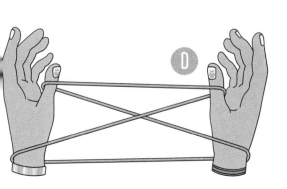

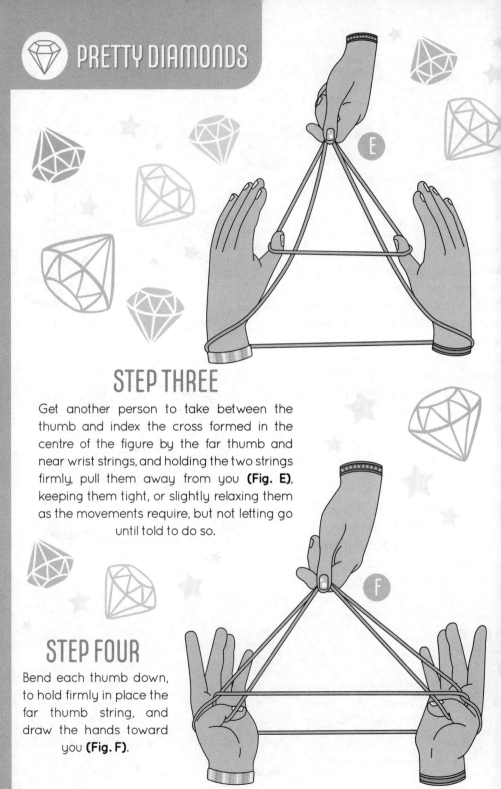

STEP THREE

Get another person to take between the thumb and index the cross formed in the centre of the figure by the far thumb and near wrist strings, and holding the two strings firmly, pull them away from you **(Fig. E)**, keeping them tight, or slightly relaxing them as the movements require, but not letting go until told to do so.

STEP FOUR

Bend each thumb down, to hold firmly in place the far thumb string, and draw the hands toward you **(Fig. F)**.

STEP FIVE

Put through the wrist loops, keeping the loops securely on the thumbs **(Fig. G)**.

STEP SIX

Turn the hands up with the palms away from you **(Fig. H, left hand)**, and slip each hand up through the thumb loop to the wrist **(Fig. H, right hand)**.

STEP SEVEN

With the back of each middle finger pick up, from below, the oblique string passing around the two strings of the wrist loop, and return the middle finger to its former position **(Fig. I)**.

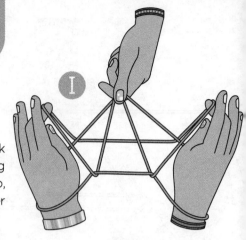

STEP EIGHT

Turn the palms slightly toward you, and bend each middle finger down over the near middle finger string, and holding the middle finger loop **(Fig. J, left hand)** tightly in position, draw each hand toward you through the wrist loop, which should be caught in passing on the back of the thumb.

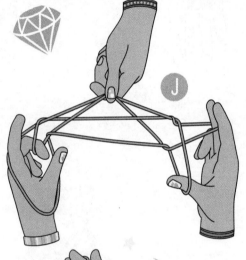

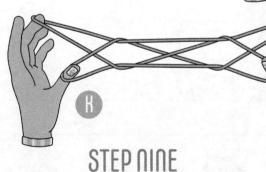

STEP NINE

Turn the palms toward each other; pull each middle finger loop further through the thumb loop, and turning the palm upward, straighten the middle finger outside of the thumb loop **(Fig. J, right hand)**.

STEP TEN

The figure is extended by spreading the thumbs and middle fingers widely apart and separating the hands **(Fig. K)**. The strings held by the second person are now released.

CELTIC KNOT

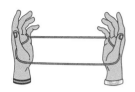

FIGURE **A**

FIGURE **B**

FIGURE **C**

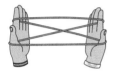

FIGURE **D**

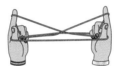

FIGURE **E**

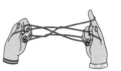

FIGURE **F**

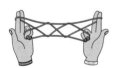

FIGURE **G**

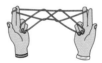

FIGURE **H**

FIGURE **I**

FIGURE **J**

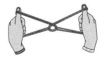

FIGURE **K**

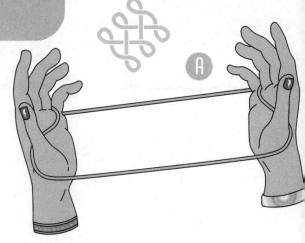

STEP ONE

Put the little fingers into the loop of string, and separate the hands. You now have a single loop on each little finger passing directly to the opposite little finger.

Turning the hands with the palms away from you, put each thumb into the little finger loop from below, and pick up on the back of the thumb the near little finger string; then, allowing the far little finger string to remain on the little finger, turn the hands with the palms facing each other, return the thumbs to their extended position, and draw the strings tight **(Fig. A)**.

STEP TWO

Pass the right index from above behind the string crossing the left palm, and as you draw the loop out, turn the right index away from you and upward **(Fig. B)**, to put a cross in the loop, and also bend the left index down, and pick up from below on the back of the finger the left near little finger string, and return the index to its position **(Fig. C)**.

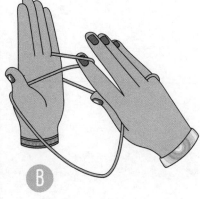

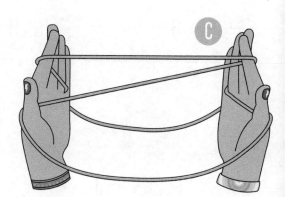

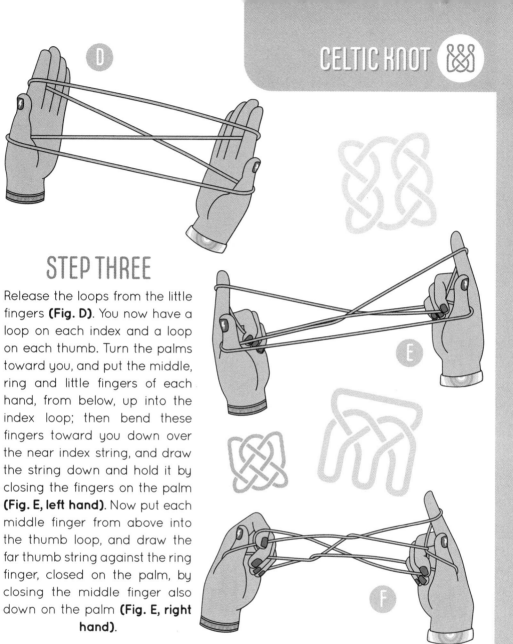

STEP THREE

Release the loops from the little fingers **(Fig. D)**. You now have a loop on each index and a loop on each thumb. Turn the palms toward you, and put the middle, ring and little fingers of each hand, from below, up into the index loop; then bend these fingers toward you down over the near index string, and draw the string down and hold it by closing the fingers on the palm **(Fig. E, left hand)**. Now put each middle finger from above into the thumb loop, and draw the far thumb string against the ring finger, closed on the palm, by closing the middle finger also down on the palm **(Fig. E, right hand)**.

STEP FOUR

Keeping carefully the string on each index, bend the index toward you over the near thumb string **(Fig. F, left hand)**; then, by moving the index away from you and upward, lift up on the tip of the finger this near thumb string, while the string already on the index slips over the tip **(Fig. F, right hand)**.

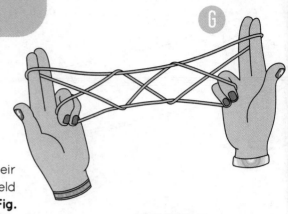

STEP FIVE

Withdraw the thumbs from their loops, and let go the string held down by each middle finger **(Fig. G)**. You now have on each hand a loop around the index and a loop held to the palm by the closed ring and little fingers.

STEP SIX

Transfer the index loops to the middle fingers, by putting each middle finger, from above, into the index loop **(Fig. H, left hand)**, withdrawing the index, and returning the middle finger to its position **(Fig. H, right hand)**.

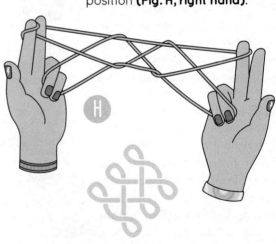

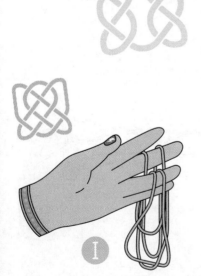

STEP SEVEN

Bring the palms close together, and hang the right middle finger loop, without twisting it, over the left middle finger; and hang the loop held on the right ring and little fingers, without twisting it, on the left ring and little fingers; withdraw the right hand **(Fig. I)**.

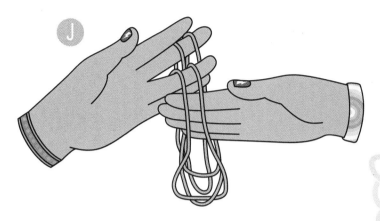

STEP EIGHT

Then put the four fingers of the right hand to the left, through the two loops hanging from the left ring and little fingers **(Fig. J)**, and closing the right fingers on the palm, take these loops off the left hand. Put the left thumb away from you into the two loops hanging from the left middle finger, and withdraw the middle finger; now put the four fingers of the left hand toward you into these loops, and close the fingers on the palm, withdrawing the thumb. Draw the strings apart. The "knot" can be tightened and loosened by rotating the wrist alternately away from you and toward you **(Fig. K)**.

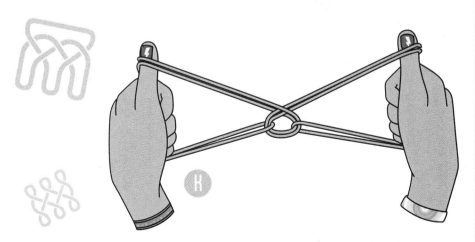

WIGWAM

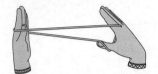

FIGURE **A**

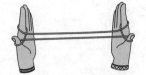

FIGURE **B**

FIGURE **C**

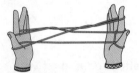

FIGURE **D**

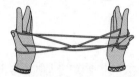

FIGURE **E**

FIGURE **F**

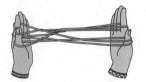

FIGURE **G**

FIGURE **H**

FIGURE **I**

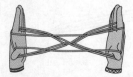

FIGURE **J**

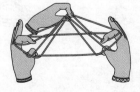

FIGURE **K**

FIGURE **L**

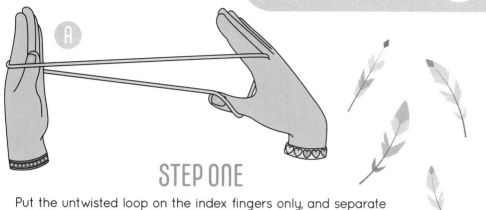

STEP ONE

Put the untwisted loop on the index fingers only, and separate the hands. Pass each thumb from below into the index loop **(Fig. A, left hand)**, bend it over the far index string and sweep it down, toward you, and up again **(Fig. A, right hand)**.

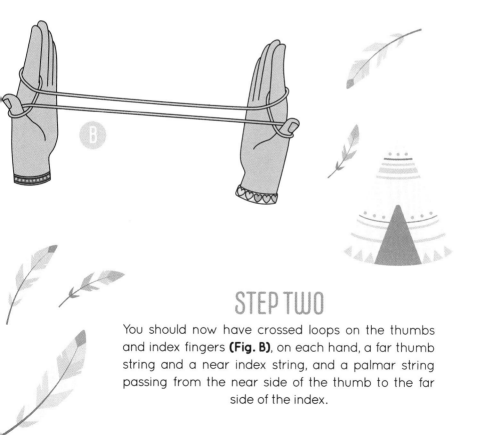

STEP TWO

You should now have crossed loops on the thumbs and index fingers **(Fig. B)**, on each hand, a far thumb string and a near index string, and a palmar string passing from the near side of the thumb to the far side of the index.

STEP THREE

Put the right index from below under this left palmar string, between the far thumb string and the near index string **(Fig. C)**, and draw the loop out on the back of the index, at the same time giving it one twist by rotating the index away from you, down, toward you, and up again **(Fig. D)**.

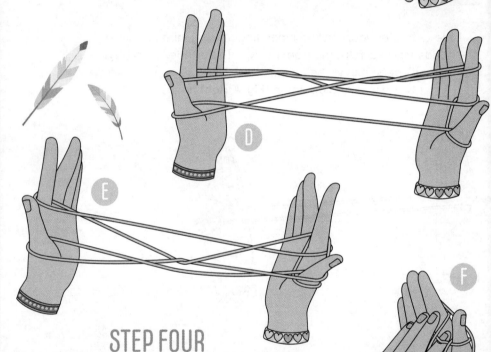

STEP FOUR

Put the right thumb from below into the right upper index loop, and separate the thumb from the index in order to make the loop wider **(Fig. E)**. Now pass the left index from above through this upper loop extended on the left thumb and index, and pick up, from below (between the lower near index string and the lower far thumb string) on the back of the left index the right palmar string **(Fig. F)**, and draw the loop out and give it one twist by rotating the left index away from you, down, toward you, and up again.

STEP FIVE

Pass the left thumb from below into the upper left index loop, and separate the thumb from the index in order to make the loop wider **(Fig. G)**.

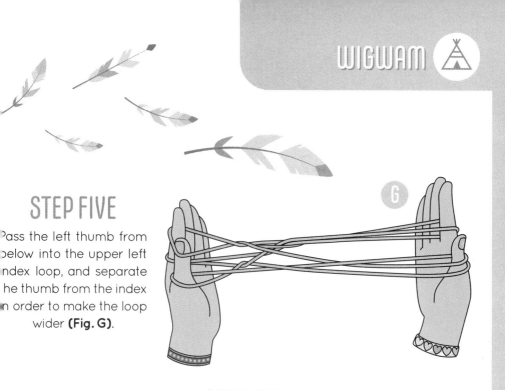

STEP SIX

Bend the right middle, ring and little fingers toward you over all the loops on the right hand, and close these fingers on the palm to hold the strings in place while you gather together, close to the left hand, between the right thumb and index all the loops on the left hand, by putting the right thumb below the loops and closing the right index down on them **(Fig. H)**.

STEP SEVEN

Now withdraw the left hand from all the loops, and with the right thumb and index turn the loops over, away from you (so that the right thumb comes on top of the loops), and put the left thumb and index back into the loop, as they were before **(Fig. I)**, except that now the left thumb loop goes on the left index and the left index loop goes on the left thumb and the loop common to both thumb and index is now the lower loop.

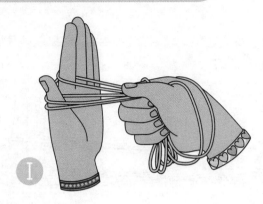

Draw the hands apart and repeat the same movement on the right hand, as follows: Bend the left middle, ring and little fingers toward you over all the loops on the left hand, and close these fingers down on the palm to hold the strings in place while you gather together, with the left thumb and index, close to the right hand, all the loops on the left hand, putting the left thumb below the loops and closing the left index down on them. Now withdraw the right hand from all the loops and with the left thumb and index turn the loops over, away from you (so that the left thumb comes on top of the loops), and put the right thumb and index back into the loops as they were before, except that now the right thumb loop goes on the right index, the right index loop goes on the right thumb and the loop common to both right thumb and index is now the lower loop.

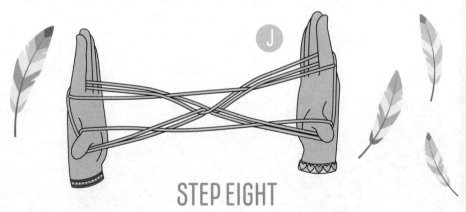

STEP EIGHT

Separate the hands and draw the strings tight **(Fig. J)**. The figure now consists of an upper string which is a single straight near index string passing on either side between the two far index strings; a lower string which is a single straight far thumb string passing, on each side, between the two near thumb strings; and double near thumb and far index strings twisted together in the centre.

STEP NINE

A second person now pulls upward the twisted strings in the centre of the figure, while you bend each index down toward you, over the near index string and each thumb away from you over the far thumb string **(Fig. K)**, and, holding these strings down, you let the other strings slip off the thumbs and index fingers. Now turn the hands with the palms down, and separate the thumbs widely from the index fingers, and the "Wigwam" is formed **(Fig. L)**.

SIX POINT STAR

Once you have mastered wigwam keep your friend on hand to help you complete this gorgeous star. The second person releases the loops which they have been holding up, and pulls out in the opposite directions the straight strings at the sides of the figure **(Fig. A)**.

JACOBS LADDER

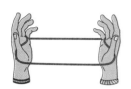

FIGURE **A**

FIGURE **B**

FIGURE **C**

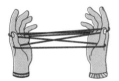

FIGURE **D**

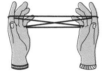

FIGURE **E**

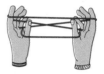

FIGURE **F**

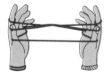

FIGURE **G**

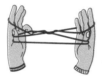

FIGURE **H**

FIGURE **I**

FIGURE **J**

FIGURE **K**

FIGURE **L**

FIGURE **M**

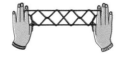

FIGURE **N**

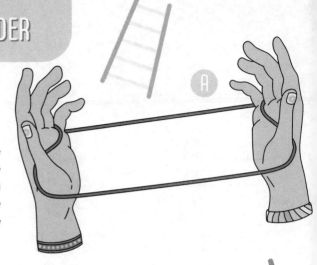

STEP ONE

Put the little fingers into the loop of string, and separate the hands. You now have a single loop on each little finger passing directly to the opposite little finger.

Turning the hands with the palms away from you, put each thumb into the little finger loop from below, and pick up on the back of the thumb the near little finger string; then, allowing the far little finger string to remain on the little finger, turn the hands with the palms facing each other, return the thumbs to their extended position, and draw the strings tight **(Fig. A)**.

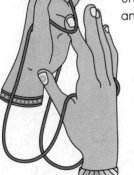

STEP TWO

Bring the hands together, and put the right index up under the string which crosses the left palm **(Fig. B)**, and draw the loop out on the back of the finger by separating the hands.

STEP THREE

Bring the hands together again, and put the left index up under that part of the string crossing the palm of the right hand which is between the strings on the right index **(Fig. C)**, and draw the loop out on the back of the left index by separating the hands.

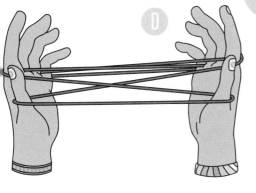

STEP FOUR

You now have a loop on each thumb, index, and little finger **(Fig. D)**. There is a near thumb string and a far little finger string passing directly from one hand to the other, and two crosses formed between them by the near little finger string of one hand becoming the far index string of the other hand, and the far thumb string of one hand becoming the near index string of the other hand.

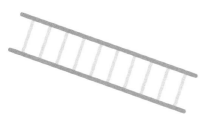

STEP FIVE

Release the loops from the thumbs and seperate the hands **(Fig. E)**.

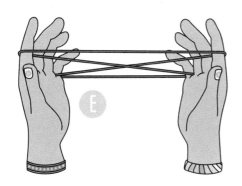

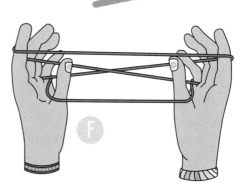

STEP SIX

Pass each thumb away from you under all the strings, and take up from below with the back of the thumb the far little finger string, and return the thumb to its former position without touching the other strings **(Fig. F)**.

STEP SEVEN

Pass each thumb away from you over the near index string, and take up, from below, with the back of the thumb the far index string and return the thumb to its former position **(Fig. G)**.

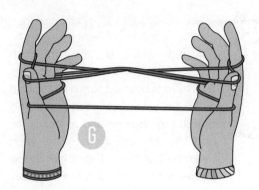

STEP EIGHT

Release the loops from the little fingers and separate the hands. Pass each little finger toward you over the near index string and take up from below on the back of the little finger the far thumb string **(Fig. H, left hand)**, and return the little finger to its former position **(Fig. H, right hand)**.

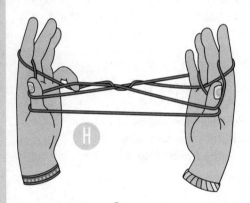

STEP NINE

Release the loops from the thumbs **(Fig. I)**.

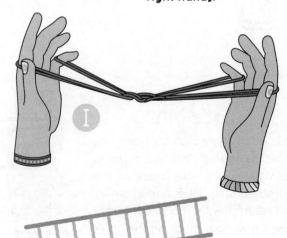

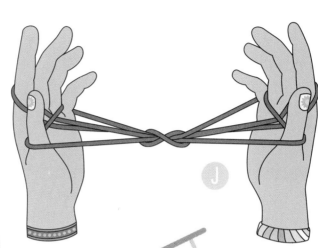

STEP TEN

Pass each thumb away from you over the index loop, and take up, from below, with the back of the thumb the near little finger string and return the thumb to its position **(Fig. J)**.

STEP ELEVEN

With the right thumb and index pick up the left near index string (close to the left index and above the left palmar string) and put it over the left thumb **(Fig. K)**.

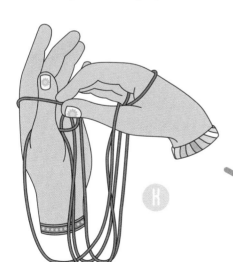

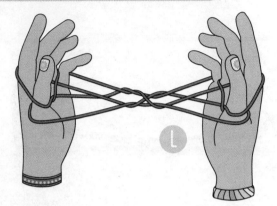

STEP TWELVE

With the left thumb and index pick up the right near index string (close to the right index and above the right palmar string) and put it over the right thumb. Separate the hands **(Fig. L)**.

STEP THIRTEEN

Bending each thumb toward the other hand and then up toward you, slip the lower near thumb string off the thumb, without disturbing the upper thumb loop **(Fig. M, left hand)**.

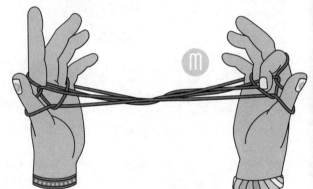

STEP FOURTEEN

Insert each index from above into the small triangle formed by the palmar string twisting around the thumb loop **(Fig. M, right hand)**, and, turning the palms down, release the loop from the little fingers; then separate the hands, turn the palms away from you, and the finished figure will appear **(Fig. N)**.

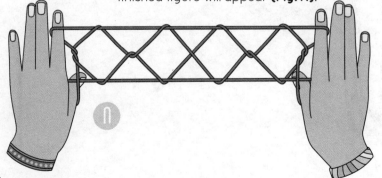